THE HAIKU PROJECT

Love in Seventeen Syllables

Julius Houndsworth

For Eliza

I am astonishingly fortunate.

For reasons I cannot fathom a young woman of exceptional beauty, grace, compassion, and persistence took a liking to me. This happened many years ago – before either of us had developed any appreciable sensibility. But whether as a consequence of the optimism of youth or a lack of judgment, she saw in me the promise of things I did not see in myself. The promise that I could move past childhood difficulty, wade through misfortune, and emerge happy and successful. She saw that I might grow into a husband and a father, and that I would find delight in both of those roles. She had more faith in me than I had in myself. In the several decades since, I've often wondered what led her to wager on our success. In the end, however, I've simply been grateful that she placed the bet.

By necessity, she and I have changed over the years. And I have also been extremely fortunate that as time has passed and each of us has matured, we've grown in tandem. She has not tired of me, nor I of her. Our relationship, borne of attraction and a shared sense of humor, has expanded. And over these years I've come to realize that she is more than one woman. She is an amalgam: companion, mother, friend, lover, teacher – all this and so much more.

These reflections led to an attempt to articulate, however clumsily, my gratitude, admiration, love and – occasionally – lust for her. I committed to writing her one poem per day – inspired by her, our life together, and my feelings for her. That commitment led to this collection.

Courtship

I

Seventeen years old

A fast food date with a girl

Life changed instantly

Waffle fries combined

Into a bag shared by two

Polynesian sauce

III

Music of great joy

Playful and harmonious

The sound of your laugh

IV

Very frightening

First asking to hold your hand

But what a payoff

V

Hesitant skater

Trying to impress a girl

Hurtles through the air

VI

When I hold your hand

I feel electricity

Ecstatic longing

VII

With your ponytail

I like to walk behind you

Watch sassy swaying

VIII

Dainty white sneakers

Ponytail swaying behind

Walking with my girl

<u>IX</u>

Walking together

Sometimes our strides coalesce

Synchronicity

<u>X</u>

Blushing, weakness, heart

fluttering – consequences

When you stroke my skin

XI

When you touch my cheek

It resonates in my toes

electricity

XII

Often seeing you

Makes the whole room go silent

While I drink you in

XIII

Without good reason

You took a chance and loved me

Impetuous youth

XIV

Unequal delight

When I hear you call my name

With love in your voice

XV

Bleary morning eyes

Quickly leap into focus

When I see you near

XVI

Unexpected date

For coffee and a pastry

Best Friday ever

XVII

When we have coffee
The caffeine doesn't wake me
So much as your kiss

XVIII

I want to kiss you

To taste the sweetness of you

Delight on my lips

XIX

Delicious kisses
Lingering on lips and tongue
Soft and warm and wet

<u>XX</u>

Honey-scented lips

Intoxicate with each touch

Instant addiction

XXI

Without your kisses
A fellow could easily
Become despondent

XXII

With every minute

By your side in the sunshine

Distance is made worse

XXIII

Sitting on a raft

Searching for tiny sunfish

I fell for you hard

XXIV

Mouse on the tent flap

Struggles to climb slick surface

Giggles from within

XXV

Melted ice cream cone

Drips flying in the warm breeze

Hot summer evening

XXVI

Arms around my waist

Leaning into gentle curves

Dancing in my dreams

XXVII

Cause of distraction

Shape of hips in clinging skirt

Metronome of joy

XXVIII

Dime-store promise ring

Dissolves in hotel hot tub

Will she still be mine?

XXIX

Stockings and silk blouse

Her question: "you wouldn't mind?"

She set the hook deep

XXX

Delicate red hairs

Covering exquisite curves

Unforgettable

XXXI

Afternoon hijinks

In a park behind a church

Glad that we weren't caught

XXXII

I seem to stay cold

You have the warmest embrace

May I sit with you?

XXXIII

I sometimes wonder
If you know how much it means
When you give your kiss

<u>XXXIV</u>

Drives with the top down
On slightly chilling evenings
Planning our future

Marriage

<u>XXXV</u>

Delicate roses

Adorn lovely gown of silk

My happiest day

XXXVI

Lightness envelops

And the world goes silent

When I see your smile

XXXVII

Tongue-tied and helpless

As you undress before me

Incorrigible

XXXVIII

Life as your husband:

A never-ending longing

To be by your side

XXXIX

Sleeping in my arms

Trusting that I will protect

Draws me in deeply

XL

Somnolent furnace

Smoldering with every breath

Burning from within

XLI

In early morning

I sometimes struggle to rise

Unless you are near

XLII

Before work travel

I think it is important

That I see you nude

XLIII

Kisses before work

Kisses when I return home

Lonely lips midday

XLIV

When we are apart

It sometimes feels like I'm lost

Outside loving arms

XLV

Bag full of carrots

With peppers, yogurt and cheese

My baby loves me

XLVI

Frequent distraction

Phantasms of your kisses

On my lonely skin

<u>XLVII</u>

With each passing year

Affection intensifies

Unwavering love

XLVIII

I carry with me

A small heart of polished stone

Memento of love

XLIX

Painted pink toenails

Cookies and milk in the sun

My girl is on break

L

Sitting in the sun
With my baby by my side
Intoxicating

LI

Sometimes I miss you

Even when you are with me

So I hold your hand

LII

Blackberry picking
Wearing a short denim dress
Look out for the thorns!

LIII

Foggy morning kiss
A promise of evening kiss
To tide me over

LIV

Kissing you softly

With intentionality

Meditative love

<u>LV</u>

Kissing in sunshine

Holding you close at breakfast

Long weekend with you

LVI

Lips as soft as love

Tender, sweet and filled with words

Strong and fierce as love

LVII

Thirty years and more
And yet you still delight me
With wit and insight

LVIII

Often I wonder

How it is that you remain

Completely ageless

LIX

Mystery of life

Why, after three long decades

You enchant me so

LX

You killed the vacuum

Strangled with lovely tresses

Hope I'm that lucky

Family Life

LXI

Holding me tightly

With snoring dog at my feet

Warm and safe and home

LXII

Chamomile flowers
Held in a fold of your skirt
Femininity

LXIII

Excited and scared

Breathing through each contraction

You made me a dad

<u>LXIV</u>

Nursing our infant
Richness and love in liquid
Factory of care

LXV

Sleepy Labrador
Napping with the mom-lady
Making me jealous

LXVI

Bigfoot might be real

Then again, might be a myth

But I'll Squatch with you

LXVII

Rustle in hedgerow

Sheepish dog with treasure

You saved a bunny

LXVIII

Phone rings in commute

Contractions – much too early

I race to your side

LXIX

Grim-faced physician
At obstetrics appointment
"don't hear a heartbeat"

LXX

I sit with our boys

Emergency room lobby

Trying not to weep

LXXI

"sometimes this happens."

Was it the hoped-for daughter?

We will never know

LXXII

Poppies in the wind

Swaying in tempests of spring

Bend and keep blooming

LXXIII

For reasons unknown
We bring life into our world
Our family complete

LXXIV

Parenting is hard
Grateful for our partnership –
We are outnumbered

LXXV

Constantly cheerful

I watch you greet the children

Unflinching kindness

LXXVI

Rabbits, baby birds

Kittens, puppies and our sons -

You're a great mom

Beauty

LXXVII

Delicate, lovely

Balancing grace with each step

Your toes make me smile

<u>LXXVIII</u>

Pale pink and dainty

Adorned with gold and jewels

Hide and seek in hair

<u>LXXIX</u>

Tousled curly hair

Styled from evening slumber

Frames exquisite face

LXXX

Burgundy buttons

Shine like rubies in the sun

Toes of perfection

LXXXI

Fabric daisies cling

To sleepy gorgeous bottom

First day of summer

LXXXII

When I see you bathe

I sometimes get distracted

And forget to breathe

LXXXIII

Delicate painted toes

Peeking from strappy sandals

May I kiss each one?

LXXXIV

It is possible

Future archaeologists

Believe you're sacred

LXXXV

Loving you deeply

With every inhalation

Lost in your beauty

LXXXVI

Saucy overalls

A gregarious redhead

BBQ cutie

Playing in the dirt

Goofy grin on lovely face

My girl in summer

<u>LXXXVIII</u>

Skin as smooth as silk

Scattered with playful freckles

Deserves to be kissed

LXXXIX

Peekaboo nipples

Dance with daisies and the cold

Causing distraction

<u>XC</u>

Outdoor fires are banned

And your beauty can ignite

Stay inside with me?

XCI

Leopard-printed shoes
Protect dainty painted toes
And attract my eyes

XCII

Delectably round

Framed with lace and enchantment

I love your bottom

Longing and Desire

XCIII

When you brush your teeth

I like to watch and admire

Beautiful shimmy

<u>XCIV</u>

Doing our laundry
I still feel titillation
Seeing your undies

<u>XCV</u>

Necktie, lingerie

Dim light and crackling fire

Seared in memory

XCVI

Your breath on my neck

A tightening in my core

Ferocious kisses

XCVII

When touching your skin

I've found it is critical

To linger a while

XCVIII

Sometimes I'll kiss you

And forget entirely

That we're not alone

<u>XCVIX</u>

A constant desire

Three decades of wanting you

May I kiss your cheek?

<u>C</u>

Legs, lusciously long

Lounging, languid and lovely.

Smooth skin and desire

<u>CI</u>

When you sleep near me
I have to remind myself:
"Don't touch her bottom!"

CII

Beautiful sisters

Equal in my affection

Tawdry and Demure

CIII

Polka dot undies

Under polka dot sundress

Fabric of my dreams

CIV

I hunger for you

To consume you utterly

Grow drunk from your flesh

CV

I want to retire

And devote all of my time

To pleasuring you

<u>CVI</u>

Delicious nipples

Framed by lovely pink circles

Make me salivate

CVII

Soap bubbles glisten

Burlesque of fragrant lather

May I help you rinse?

CVIII

Incessant longing

Addiction to your caress

Side-effects of you

CVIX

The warmth of your mouth

On the coolness of my skin

Please kiss me again!

CX

Tempting and lovely

Aphrodite in the flesh

Divine sacrament

<u>CXI</u>

Letting things simmer

Always enhances pleasure

Exponentially

CXII

Delicious nipples
Dancing on my hungry lips
Nightly fantasy

CXIII

Luscious, supple, soft

Bounding free from pink brassiere

Tawdry on my mind

CXIV

Moonlight on your skin

Compound curves in porcelain

Haunt me in my dreams

CXV

Constant distraction

An all-consuming longing

To be one with you

CXVI

Sweet-scented lotion

On the cheeks of your bottom

Drags me into lust

CXVII

Starry flecks of glitter

Lounge in secluded valley

Beckoning me in

CXVIII

Words – lustful, filthy

Spring free from beautiful lips

Quickening my pulse

<u>CXIX</u>

Espresso kisses

Warm and sweet and inviting

Bing me to my knees

CXX

Let me kiss your feet

I promise that I'll stop there

'less I change my mind

CXXI

Warm sudsy water
Pressing naked skin to skin
Best bathtub ever

Contentment

CXXII

Sleeping by your side

Often I'll wake, see you, and

Fall in love again

CXXIII

Morning comes too soon

But when your love is near me

I wake easily

<u>CXXIV</u>

Contented and warm

Shaking off cobwebs of sleep

Waking by your side

CXXV

The scent of your sleep

Lingering on your pillow

My favorite smell

CXXVI

Lazy fall evenings

Cinnamon cappuccino

A glider and you

CXXVII

Cinnamon dusting

On top of morning coffee

Our weekend is here

CXXVIII

Little white sneakers

With a blue tag on the back

Remind me of you

CXXIX

Arms encircling me

Hold me as my dreams begin

Peaceful slumber deep

<u>CXXX</u>

Circle wiggle toes

Nonchalantly distract me

While my coffee cools

CXXXI

Walking hand in hand

Laughing together in time

Heart swells with gladness

CXXXII

Coffee and bagels

Overlooking a duck pond

Saturday with you

CXXXIII

Lemon blueberry

With my weekend companion

Pastry optional

CXXXIV

Morning espresso

Overlooking the water

Lotto not needed

<u>CXXXV</u>

Crisp evening air

The sweet sound of your laughter

Walks with you at dusk

CXXXVI

Memories of you
Come flooding into my mind
When I think of joy

CXXXVII

Giggling and playing

Three decades of silliness

Love wrapped in laughter

CXXXVIII

Happiness, delight,

Warmth and comfort surround me

When thinking of you

CXXXIX

Pajama coffee

On a glider on the porch

Starts my day with joy

CXL

Summer draws to close

Sadness mitigated by

Plans to cuddle you

CXLI

Fall geese on the wing

Announce the arrival of

Sweater snuggle time

CXLII

Stews and roasted meats

Baking bread, cookies and pies

You make the best smells

CXLIII

Waking by your side

Bleary-eyed and contented

Happy to be home

CXLIV

Memories flood back
Of acid-washed jeans and malls
When you hold my hand

CXLV

Hearing your heartbeat

Feeling the warmth of your touch

Lying in your lap

CXLVI

Unexpected rain

Derails planned camping trip

Watch storm and snuggle

CXLVII

Holding you closely

With sleeping dogs on the bed

Midafternoon nap

CXLVIII

Garden, shop and bench

Small house with beautiful view

Dreams of our future

CXLIX

Fall arriving soon
And with it, strong memories
Crisp evening walks

CL

As I breathe you in

Holding you while you're sleeping

All the world grows still